W9-ACW-855

WORDS IN PAIN

WORDS

CONFERENCES ON THE SEVEN

FIDES PUBLISHERS Notre Dame, Indiana

IN PAIN

LAST WORDS OF CHRIST

Bishop John Wright

Illustrations by Mary Ellen Ebling

Royalties from the sale of this book go entirely to the Catholic Institute of Pittsburgh for works of charity, education and religion.

Nihil Obstat:
Louis J. Putz, C.S.C.
University of
Notre Dame

Imprimatur:
Leo A. Pursley, D.D.
Bishop of Fort Wayne-
South Bend, Indiana

These conferences were first preached at St. Clement's Shrine, Boston, in the Three Hours Devotion. They were subsequently repeated in the Cathedral of the Holy Cross and St. James Church, Boston, at other Good Friday services. In their revised form, as here presented, they were preached in St. Paul's Cathedral, Worcester, Good Friday' 1952, and as a Lenten course at St. Paul's Cathedral, Pittsburgh, 1960. Many of the points developed in them doubtless echo the sermons, heard or read, of much more original preachers, but, drawn from the common patrimony of the faithful, they are offered for the instruction or consolation of all who care to share them.

✠ John Wright,

Bishop of Pittsburgh

O, but they say the tongues of dying men enforce attention like deep harmony. Where words are scarce, they are seldom spent in vain, for they breathe truth that breathe their words in pain. . . .

Richard II, act II, scene i.

Prologue

The First Word

The Second Word

The Third Word

The Fourth Word

The Fifth Word

The Sixth Word

The Seventh Word

PROLOGUE

Dignus est agnus qui occisus est. . . . The Lamb that was slain is worthy to receive power, and divinity, and wisdom, and strength, and honour, and glory, and benediction. (Apoc. 5, 12).

The crucifixion of Jesus Christ took place a long time ago and far away from here. It is an old and familiar story, yet it would scarcely be worthy of mention after all these centuries if the Crucified had been only another victim of man's inhumanity to man; if He, like countless estimable men, had been once falsely judged, once cruelly rejected, once unjustly put to death.

Despite all efforts of popular historians to number Jesus among the great martyrs of *human* history, the Nazarene still soars in dignity above human standards and claims an homage apart. He was no mere lover of His nation, one of many to offer His life as part of the price of His people's freedom; He was no mere philosopher, one of scores who have accepted death for bearing partial witness to the truth; He was no mere philanthropist, slain for His noble deeds and misunderstood in His higher purposes. Neither can His death be set down as the event of a day, taking place in an hour, at a defined place. The event we commemorate during this holy season is not merely something which happened once on a hill outside Jerusalem. It is something which everlastingly happens, everywhere. The crucifixion of Jesus Christ is the central event of history. All other events take on new meaning from it, those before straining toward it, those since living by it.

Sensitive historians inevitably come to recognize something, at least of the centrality of the Cross in human history. It was the great German historian Harnack who wrote: "There is no other fact in all history which mankind needs so much to have brought home to it as this: A man by the name of Jesus Christ once stood in our midst." Harnack undoubtedly referred to what he would have called "the historical Jesus" rather than to the Christ of theology; to the Man Jesus rather than to the Son of God. Yet the ultimate reason for that centrality of Christ to which Harnack bears witness is not historical, but theological. Christ and His Cross explain history, but history offers no explanation of them. The real reason for the centrality in human affairs of Christ and His Cross is set forth in a theological truth revealed early in St. John's Gospel: ". . . AS MOSES LIFTED UP THE SERPENT IN THE DESERT, SO MUST THE SON OF MAN BE LIFTED UP:

THAT WHOSOEVER BELIEVETH IN HIM, MAY NOT PERISH; BUT MAY HAVE LIFE EVERLASTING. FOR GOD SO LOVED THE WORLD, AS TO GIVE HIS ONLY BEGOTTEN SON; THAT WHOSOEVER BELIEVETH IN HIM, MAY NOT PERISH, BUT MAY HAVE LIFE EVERLASTING." (3, 14-16). It is, then, of fundamental importance, if we would understand human history, for us to remember that a man by the name of Jesus once stood in our midst; but it is even more basic, if we would understand the place of Jesus in history, that we be mindful of the word of St. Paul: "FOR GOD INDEED WAS IN CHRIST, RECONCILING THE WORLD TO HIMSELF." (2 Cor., 5, 19).

This is the essential thing to remember about the Cross—that God was at work upon it, not man alone. A human nature died on Calvary, but all of the significance and efficacy of that death derive from the fact that the human nature so dying belonged to a Person Who was Divine. Had Jesus Christ been but a man, the Cross would have been a tragedy, as the brutal murder of the innocent must always be tragic. But the crucified Christ was God, the eternal Son, acting in and through the human nature which He had taken upon Himself when He became incarnate by the mysterious action of the Holy Ghost in the most pure Virgin Mary. "True God of true God . . . consubstantial with the Father, by Whom all things were made. Who for us men, and for our salvation, came down from heaven. And was incarnate by the Holy Ghost of the Virgin Mary: and was made man. For us also was He crucified. . . ." Thus these twenty centuries have Christians sung at Mass their debt to Jesus Christ.

No moment in the life of Jesus Christ has been so graven in the memory of those who love Him as the moment of His crucifixion. Strange thing: that the event in His life most cherished by His followers should be the moment of His most utter humiliation; that the sign and symbol of those who think Him God should be the instrument designed by His enemies to break Him forever; that every effort to make Him loathsome should have made Him the Hero of the ages, so that artists have always preferred to portray Him crucified, *that the beauty of His countenance might never be Hidden from His own; that the wounds and woe wherein He wrote His love might be known to all the people He died to redeem.*

Why do we find Him so beautiful in death Who should never have died? Why is His Cross so ardently kissed, so proudly borne aloft? Why? unless it be that, however we may speak of the *tragedy* of Calvary, every Christian knows in his heart of hearts that Calvary was a *triumph;* that there is some secret victory here.

So we invite you in these meditations to consider less the horrors of Calvary, and more its glory. The traditional emphasis on the human sufferings of Calvary seems to be due to the notion that Jesus was somehow defeated, even if only momentarily, on the Cross. He was *not*—not for one moment. His whole Passion was an unbroken victory of the merciful ingenuity of God over the pathetic malice of men. We must not think of Easter and the Resurrection as compensations, as it were, for the failures Christ suffered on Good Friday; we must recognize that Sunday is all of one piece with Friday. It is the final scene in a series of triumphs. In one sense, we might almost say, Easter is less wonderful than Good Friday—something of an anti-climax—for surely it is less wonderful to break the bonds of physical death and give back life to one man, than it is to break, as Jesus did on Friday, the bonds of moral death and give back the life of their souls to the unremembered dead, to the unnumbered living and to the countless hosts of the unborn who would, in their turn, need redemption.

Even if we forget for a moment (which we cannot do) that the dying Jesus is still God and cannot ultimately be defeated, we must see in Calvary the triumph of every human virtue over the most desperate onslaught of every human vice. Usually in life, even in the most virtuous lives, goodness tends to be obscure, rarely rising above an unattractive mediocrity. In the Passion of the Man Jesus goodness attained the heights of a commanding beauty. The moral beauty of Jesus takes the form of an absolute unselfishness, a resignation which gives the condemned man a calm and compelling dignity. At the moment of His arrest Jesus feared not at all for Himself, but only for His followers.

Almost eagerly He asks His pursuers: "Whom seek ye?" "Jesus of Nazareth." "I am He! Let these others go!"

Nor should this calm seem strange to us. It was not by historical chance nor against His will that Jesus died on Calvary. He delivered Himself up, says St. Peter, by the determinate counsel and foreknowledge of God. All of His ascetical teaching to others presupposes the freedom with which He accepted death on His own Cross: "If any man will come after Me, let him deny himself, and take up his cross and follow Me." "No one can take My life from Me." Thus He proclaimed the freedom with which He died. "I alone have the power to lay it down and the power to take it up again!" Not even His human nature endured anything out of necessity and fatal compulsion; His death and all of the sufferings incidental to it were His own free choice. This it was that rendered His passion so meritorious, so full of mercy and goodness: that He did freely offer Himself, all for the honor of God and the sanctification of men. Thus that death, which His enemies contrived with other purposes and in mere malice, He freely made the instrument of His own sublime ends, of His most excelling charity.

Nor did fear of the world or its powers impel Him to His choice: it was not after His Resurrection, but before His death, that Christ bade His followers be of good heart whate'er befell Him. "Have confidence," He said, "for I have overcome the world." Neither was it forgetfulness of His great dignity which made possible His choice; at no moment was Christ unconscious of His divinity. In the Garden of Olives He was mindful that the angels of Heaven are His servants. Before Caiphas He claimed for Himself the dignity of the Son of Man and proclaimed that He would one day come to judge as surely as that day He was judged. Even in His last hours Jesus, to the eyes of others so spent, so frustrated, remained still the conscious Lord of life, of the future, and of death. Lord of life, He paused en route to judgment to heal the ear of Malchus. Lord of the future, He foretold to the women of Jerusalem the bitter fate of their unborn and unbelieving descendants, and for these He bade the women weep. Lord of death,

He held that creature off as long as He wished, nor let it approach until He had completed the work He had set for Himself in every detail, and precisely as He had willed it.

Then *why* did Jesus freely will to suffer and so to die? The answer is quite simple, and it adds new lustre to the glory of Calvary and the triumph of the Cross. It is writ large in every page of the Gospels and Epistles; it is the echoed theme of all our heritage of Christian meditation and preaching: Jesus chose to suffer and die *because He loved us*. Loyalty unto death is the ultimate proof of love: there is no greater love, Jesus said, than dying for one's friends. *And Jesus died for us.*

"Nails were never enough to hold the God-Man fastened to the Cross had love not held Him captive first!" Love made Him freely choose to die; love made Him eager to use for us His divine freedom to die. Indeed, He was impatient to die. "I have desired this with a great desire," He said of His last reunion with His Apostles. All His life He had hailed the hour of His death as *His* hour. "The hour cometh," He repeats constantly to His disciples; and when it is at last only minutes away, He doesn't wait for His enemies to come and claim Him: "Arise," He invites His friends, "Let us go hence to meet them!" It is with the radiant eagerness of a bridegroom, rather than with the hesitant step of a defeated man, that Jesus went forth to His death. Captured, He not only makes no resistance, but He repudiates Peter's defence; He orders His Apostle to put aside his sword, and asks this strange proud question: "The chalice which My Father hath given Me—shall I not drink it?" as if to rebuke any effort made to deny Him the privilege of dying for us, so to speak, with all His heart and soul.

So it is almost with longing that Jesus embraced His Cross; this was the weapon of His combat, this the pledge of His love, this the keynote of His triumph. St. Andrew, mindful of his Master's death, wept for sheer joy when he beheld his own cross. Can we, then, wonder that our Saviour, receiving His Cross, exulted at the thought of those for whom His love would prove fruitful, thanks to the Cross; of those who would bear patiently their crosses out of love for His Cross; of the glory He would win for His Father eternally and the grace He would win for His brethren forever by His few hours on the Cross.

Ah, no! Romantics and others of little faith! Weep for your sins that required of God's love so much, so very much! But weep no tears over this tomb as if it hid defeat or imprisoned failure. Jesus Christ came into the world as Sanctity Incarnate to sanctify the world. Nowhere was His Sanctity more marked with grandeur than on the Cross; by nothing did He sanctify as He did by the Cross. No faith in Him is firmer than that learned at the foot of His Cross; no hope is more buoyant than that inspired by the sight of His Cross; no charity more ardent than that communicated with the love of His Cross. How call that Cross a failure which, keylike in the hands of Christ, opened the gates twixt earth and heaven to give Christ so many brethren there; opened the gates twixt heaven and earth to give us so many imitators of Christ to guide us finally to Him: so many Benedicts and Bernards, so many Xaviers and Dominics, so many

Catherines and Theresas, so many Marthas and so many Marys in fulfillment of Christ's own prophecy: "I, if I be lifted up from the earth, will draw all things to Myself."

THE FIRST WORD

Father, forgive them, for they know not what they do! (Luke 23, 24).

And I looked for one that would grieve together with me, but there was none: and for one that would comfort me, and I found none. (Psalm 68, 21).

The revolt against Jesus Christ on Calvary was total. It spread its contagion to all the human family and through it to the whole material world, so that even inanimate nature had somehow joined in the conspiracy against its Maker and Redeemer. His material creation furnished the flares which guided the malignant who went forth to seize Him; metal of its yielding was hammered into the manacles, the nails and the spear which mutilated His adorable flesh; it was woven into the cords which held Him captive and the whips which tore His sacred back; it took the dye of the mocking purple that ridiculed His Kingship; its thorns dug His beloved head, and of its bitterness they made Him drink.

But the principal rebel on Calvary against His Maker and His Christ is man, all men. Pilate, representing the power and prestige of that Rome which governed the known world, had sent Him to His death. The Jewish priests were there to speak in the name of the human side of religion their word of repudiation. The Greeks were present to add their urbane and cultured word of contempt. The brutal work of beating Him and hammering Him to the Cross,—well, Caesar's soldiery was there for that, the representatives of the barbarous colonial world of the day; Persians, perhaps Numidians, Gauls, Teutons. Every race gave its contribution of malign genius to His crucifixion.

All social classes, all vocational groups, every level of society afforded its quota of hatred and evil ingenuity. Skilled lawyers, civil and canon, wove the plot, anticipated every eventuality, directed the intrigue, instigated the process, primed the witnesses, forced the decisions. A king made Jesus the sport of his decadent court; two high-priests twisted the Scriptures to prove Him blasphemous. The social aristocracy of the Sadducees spat at Him their contempt; the intellectual aristocracy of the Pharisees played cleverly with His phrases to prove Him a fool. The maidservant baited His followers; the soldiery made merry over His confusion; and the proletariat, united for once with the classes, cried out their ratification of the mighty's decision to crucify Him. Even the outlaw elements of society were represented by at least one condemned thief to curse Him.

"I looked for one that would grieve together with Me, but there was none: and for one that would comfort Me, and I found none." Could anything more total than the rebellious repudiation of Jesus be imagined, anything more universal than the indifference of the world to His woe? Nothing could have been more all-embracing.

Yet one thing is; and it, too, was present on Calvary as present it must always be wherever Jesus is present: the merciful compassion of Christ. If the universal hatred of the world found its formula in the cry, *Crucify Him, crucify Him!* the compassion of Christ found a formula scarcely less brief, *Father, forgive them, for they know not what they do!* Jesus kept repeating this, tradition tells us, all through the dreadful time needed to strip Him, to stretch Him on His Cross, to nail Him there, and to lift His bleeding body high. It was a prayer uttered primarily for those who were actually engaged in the murderous work of His execution, those concerning whom St. Paul was later to write, "If they had known, they would never have crucified the Lord of Glory!" But we, too, were present in that prayer, for we, too, were involved in that repudiation; indeed we involve ourselves further whenever we prefer sin to Christ. That is the tragic fact which explains why, as each Good Friday we climb in spirit Calvary's hill, we have the strange sense of having been there before, of having played some part in the iniquities which have given Calvary its terrible power permanently to haunt the memory of man.

Thank God, we were also somehow present in that prayer of forgiveness, in the commemoration Our High Priest made of each of us even before our birth, in the most holy memento which Jesus made for sinners in that Sacrifice of the Mass He offered on the altar of the Cross: "Father, forgive them! They know not what they do!"

Whatever their implications, however, Christ's words applied primarily to that crowd on Calvary who, with varying degrees of immediacy, tormented Him as He was dying and for whom, in this first word, Jesus made excuse. How shall we explain the change into a mob, seeking His blood, of a population which, in great numbers at least, had made a holiday of His entry into Jerusalem scarcely a week before? The question is not merely historical; it has a burning topical interest. For how shall we explain this identical phenomenon in our own day, when peoples who hailed, it seems but yesterday, the peace of Christ, are now so easily moved to cry for war? How shall we explain that the good people of Christian countries, people who have in processions in the past few years acclaimed the Eucharistic Christ, are now brought to follow men who condemn Christ and devote their best energies to wiping out His name from the hearts of those who love Him?

Solon, the Greek sage and lawgiver, said of his Athenians that each of them, considered separately, was as shrewd as a fox, but that united they were hopelessly obtuse; they never knew what they did. The Romans used to say, "Senators are such good men that it is difficult to explain how the senate does such harm." They seemed not to know what they were doing. In our day there is much said and written about the special psychology of the crowd, the peculiar laws of mass-suggestion that operate in an assembly, or even a nation, and impel it to do with pride and exultation something of which any single member, if he tried, would probably prove morally incapable and certainly thoroughly ashamed. The cry of a fanatic, the word of an orator, some gesture charged with emotional significance, and a people who were a moment before women on their way to market, children on their way to play, men on the way to work, become an unreasoning herd, capable of the most brutal and reprehensible deeds of violence—deeds almost so involuntary that each goes home, when finally the stampede is over, with a nameless sense of guilt, asking himself: Whatever happened? No one seemed to know what he was doing.

The mobs who clamored about Jesus from the praetorium to Calvary were just such mobs as might have included us; there were conservative people as well as irresponsibles; friends of the government and critics; people who probably served God and people who never gave Him a thought; good people and people not-so-good, a typical mob. Yet when here and there a voice said: "The Jews want Pilate to crucify Him", the mob took up the refrain: "Crucify Him! Crucify Him!" When someone said, whether wistfully or bitterly (who knows?): "Once I heard Him say that if the Temple were destroyed, He could rebuild it in three days," that word whirled about in the mob like a spark in reeds until it was roared back at Him: "THOU THAT DESTROYEST THE TEMPLE AND BUILDEST IT AGAIN IN THREE DAYS, SAVE THYSELF!" Perhaps someone said in kind remembrance: "He always trusted in God; I heard Him say He was the Son of God,"—this, too, the mob caught up: "A man here heard Him say that He was the Son of God; the crucified one trusted in God! He trusted in God! THEN LET GOD DELIVER HIM, IF GOD WILL HAVE HIM!" Perhaps some women whispered among themselves: "I know people who lived once in Naim . . . I knew a soldier who said that his centurion's daughter . . . I heard about ten lepers . . . My brother knew a blind man . . . This Christ saved a widow's son . . . He saved a cripple . . . There was a public sinner . . . He saved her!" HE SAVED OTHERS—now the mob has made its great simplification — "THEN LET HIM SAVE HIMSELF! LET HIM COME DOWN FROM THE CROSS, AND THEN WE'LL BELIEVE HIM!"

And Jesus kept repeating, "Father, forgive them! For they know not what they do!"

Twenty centuries have gone by and still they do not know! The wrath of the stupid is still unloosed against Christ. In pagan nations and in lands called Christian, in backward nations and in lands called progressive, Christ in His Church is still led forth to crucifixion. Still the mob, fascinated by His power to suffer, to die, and to endure, seizes on every phrase He utters through His Church and hurls it at His head.

"FATHER, FORGIVE THEM! FOR THEY KNOW NOT WHAT THEY DO!" Still through His Church Jesus, offering no reproof, making no complaint, echoes His first word of Calvary, the word which has come spontaneously to Christian lips since holy Stephen, the first martyr in time and dignity after Christ, cried out above the shouts of his executioners the prayers we must make for our enemies if we would ourselves be forgiven: "LORD JESUS, LAY NOT THIS SIN TO THEIR CHARGE!"

We cannot pretend fully to understand the mystery of mercy so great as that of Christ. We think it wond'rous that Christ prayed for His enemies, a thing we find well-nigh impossible to do. But Christ did something far more wonderful, far more unselfish even than that: CHRIST DIED FOR HIS ENEMIES. We think it most exemplary, most moving and marvelous, if men are willing to die for those who love them, to put others who are their friends before themselves. Christ put even enemies before Himself, and thus He found it easy to forgive them. By His divine craft, His sacred charity, He made their final crime against Him, their conspiracy to murder Him, the means by which all their lesser crimes against Him would be forgiven His enemies . . . and us.

THE SECOND WORD

This day thou shalt be with Me in Paradise. (Luke 23, 43.)

The mob, surfeited with the whole affair, was beginning now to scatter. The chosen friends of Jesus, save for a noble few, were in hiding. The soldiers, poor tools, were whiling away the time until He should be dead by casting lots for the remnants of His shabby garments. With His blood, whatever of human life had not been beaten out of Him was ebbing rapidly away. Now surely the victory of His enemies is complete; surely now no one will be seduced by Him. Now He has done His last wonder, and we need not expect to hear His name again. Poor man! And yet. . . .

"Jesus!" There is agony in the voice, yet a strange buoyancy. "Jesus!"

It is one of the thieves who were crucified with Him. What can he possibly want of the wretched Nazarene?

"Lord, remember me when Thou comest into Thy Kingdom!"

O, what miracle is this? There have been leaders who could command followers so long as their fortunes ran high. There have been leaders who could retain through a crisis the followers who had been with them in their happier days and who could in crisis reasonably hope for the return of prosperity. But this Leader was such that, even when His enemies had done their worst, a crucified bandit, who had probably never seen Him before and had only a mocking inscription to tell him His name, looked into the dying eyes of Jesus and saluted Him as a king!

Let us read from St. Luke the five short verses which tell this story; five short verses out of all the thousands which comprise our Scriptures, and yet which have brought so much consolation to so many millions.

"AND ONE OF THE ROBBERS BLASPHEMED HIM, SAYING: IF THOU BE CHRIST, SAVE THYSELF, AND US.

BUT THE OTHER ANSWERING, REBUKED HIM SAYING: DOST THOU NOT FEAR GOD, SEEING THOU ART UNDER THE SAME CONDEMNATION?

AND WE INDEED JUSTLY, FOR WE RECEIVE THE DUE REWARD OF OUR DEEDS: BUT THIS MAN HATH DONE NO EVIL.

AND HE SAID TO JESUS: LORD, RE-

MEMBER ME WHEN THOU SHALT COME INTO THY KINGDOM.

AND JESUS SAID TO HIM: AMEN, I SAY TO THEE, THIS DAY THOU SHALT BE WITH ME IN PARADISE." (Luke 23, 39-43.)

How many parents, heartsore over the discovery of a criminal among their children, have searched out these lines to trace in them some hope! How many prisoners have read this story of Dismas, a man who for all but a few moments of his life was one of them, and, insensible perhaps to every other divine perfection, have fixed their hopes on this manifestation of the divine attribute which they hope God will exercise toward them. Which of us dares deny that he too shares that burning hope?

With all of our equipment for study and prayer and meditation, we know so little about God's true nature that we set great store by every little clue that reason or revelation gives us concerning Him. A man who perhaps himself hoped that in Divinity great mercy would be found—the turbulent and mysterious Abelard—pointed once to a tree lying sawed through the middle beside his companion and himself. "See that dark ring there," he said; "it goes up and down the whole inner length of the tree, but we see it only where the tree is cut across. Christ's life was like that: it was the bit of God that we could see!" We are grateful that so many of the flashing insights into God's nature afforded us by incidents in the life of Christ give grounds for the hope that His loving mercy is indeed above all His works.

So we are thankful for this second word because it tells us so much we had hoped would be true about God and His Christ. It tells us His wondrous power to captivate those hearts which hide any trace of potential kinship with Himself, and what heart does not? Wonderful was the conversion of Mary Magdalen, whose heart of flesh became a spiritual heart under the spell of Christ, of His generosity to her and His courtesy. Wonderful was the conversion of Paul, who turned in a trice from a narrow, nationalistic fanatic to the most universal-minded, the most illumined, the most persuasive of the Apostles. Magdalen had seen men change their lives for Christ; Paul had seen at least one man die for Christ, calling out to

Jesus as his God. But surely, Christ destitute and pinned to a cross could scarcely be generous to a thief; Christ bleeding and broken could hardly remember to be courteous; Christ had no signs of His majesty here, and such as here called out to Him did so to curse Him and call Him a fraud. O truly magnetic power of Jesus, which makes itself felt though it be buried deep under ignominy and confusion!

Now if what Christ says in this second word shows forth His mercy and His power, His very way of saying it bears witness to the nature and quality of His love. O Catholic Christians, who profess especially to love God and yet whose love for Him is so often matter-of-fact, almost impersonal, a thing of cool duty and dull routine, meditate this day on the intensely personal love which Jesus Christ bears toward you. It shines through every phrase Christ uttered to your kinsman, the Good Thief, on Calvary. "Lord," said the thief, "remember me when Thou shalt come into Thy Kingdom!" Just *remember* me. This is all the thief dared ask: when someday, God knows when, Your Kingdom comes, I shall be content if only You *remember* me! But Jesus is not content to leave it so: He doesn't promise simply to remember him. *"Thou shalt be with Me in My paradise."* His love brooks no delay: not sometime, don't know when, don't know how, but *this day* thou shalt be with Me in paradise.

Mark the simplicity of Christ's mode of speaking, its personal character, its directness: "VERILY I SAY TO *THEE,* THIS DAY THOU SHALT BE WITH ME IN PARADISE." The love of Jesus Christ (and Christ is God) is a deeply personal love for each one of us. He does not love us as a group, vaguely and generically. He does not love us because He loves humanity: it is quite the other way round. Jesus loves humanity because intensely, personally, passionately, He loves the individual soul of every man, woman and child whom humanity includes. Who would not love a God who first loves us so much?

We study this second word, too, because it teaches us about the thief, that we may imitate him. For some time before he acknowledged Christ, this man, for all his torments and his woe, had been striving to silence the bitter attacks of his companion on Jesus. He found breath and strength to rebuke the other thief, saying, "Dost thou not even fear God, seeing that thou art under the same sentence? And ourselves indeed justly, for we are receiving the fitting rewards of our deeds; but this man hath done naught amiss!"

O ye who wonder how best to come to Christ, note well the order in these stages of conversion: first there is a simple recognition of the ordinary human rights of an ordinary man like himself; and then hardly has the thief thus acted with true humanity than a great grace is given to him—that of believing that this dying man whom he had defended, this wretched condemned outcast, was the Christ, the Son of God, the Author of life, the King of Heaven. Having thus passed from natural decency to supernatural faith, he receives immediately the promise of heaven: "THIS DAY THOU SHALT BE WITH ME IN PARADISE."

"Tell! bold but blessed thief
Who in a trice
Slipped into paradise,
And in plain day

Stole heaven away . . .
What trick didst thou invent
To compass thy intent?
What arms?
What charms?
'Love and belief!'
Tell, bold but blessed thief,
How couldst thou read
A crown upon that head?
How see through dross
A Kingdom on a Cross?
How couldst thou come to spy
God in a man about to die?
What light?
What sight?
'The sight of grief!
I knew God by his pain!
And by that sight
I saw the light;
Thus did my grief
For Him beget relief . . .
So learn this rule from me:
Pity thou Him and He will pity thee!' "

This word detains us finally because of what it tells us concerning the Church. Just as the thief was the greater saint because he believed in Christ when the motives for belief were least, so those who love the Church and believe in the Christ-life of the Church when least its life is apparent, deserve best at God's hands. It is easy to believe in Catholicism and to love it when it is the inspiration of artists; when it is enjoying a golden age of sanctity and prosperity. It is easy to believe in the Church when she is transfigured in her saints or venerable in her more learned pontiffs and doctors. But when she is persecuted and reviled, outlawed and out-of-fashion,—then glorious is the faith of those who still love her! When she is eclipsed by the deficiencies of her leaders, or has become weak in the infidelity of her followers, then should we reverence the extraordinary holiness of those who still cleave to her and seek Paradise from her. These holy souls, like the good thief, the only man in history infallibly promised Heaven while he was still in the body, see Christ in torment, yet adore Him as if He were in glory; see

Christ on the Cross and pray to Him as if He were in Heaven; see Christ crucified yet call Him King; see Christ unable to hold on to the life of this world yet, with wondrous faith, dare ask Him for the life of the world to come.

Still to Christ in His Church the taunt of the other thief, the hardened of heart, is made: "IF THOU BE CHRIST, SAVE THYSELF AND US!" Still some are found to make their own the reproach to Christ by which our high-priests, our scribes, our rulers, still try to rationalize their crimes in terms of Christ's failure: *You talked of a new social order and while there was peace we refused to listen. Now that thanks to our intrigues, the world is at war and chaos howls around us, give us that social order and we will believe you.* Or: *if you were divine, why didn't you prevent the war? Why didn't you make us pure . . . honest . . . wise . . . loyal . . . merciful . . . cooperative? . . . if you are of God?*

And the Church—Christ in the world—answers nothing to these cynical taunts.

But, should one man, one family, one nation, rise above the cynicism of the world to offer her faith and to ask of her the only help she pretends to be able to give, the Church still offers—not a new political system by which yesterday's prisoners become tomorrow's princes, not a new economic regime in which today's paupers become future millionaires—but the only gift within her power: *Paradise,* the fatherland of kings and criminals alike, if only they learn to love God.

THE THIRD WORD

Now there stood by the cross of Jesus, His mother, and His mother's sister, Mary of Cleophas, and Mary Magdalen. When therefore Jesus had seen His mother and the disciple standing whom He loved, He saith to His mother: *Woman, behold thy son.* After that, He saith to the disciple: *Behold thy mother.* And from that hour, the disciple took her to his own. (John 19, 25-27).

We turn now from sinners to saints, from those who cannot yet be rid of Christ, though they hate Him, to those who are free to leave Him but will not because they love Him more than life itself. Does it not seem strange to you that the first thought of Jesus should have been for His murderers, taking the form of an anxiety lest they be punished for the crimes they were doing against Him? That His second thought should have been for a man who was, in one sense, a total stranger; and that only when He had comforted this poor thief, did He think of His own flesh and blood, His Mother, and of the disciple whom most especially He cherished as His friend?

Does it disturb you? Before you answer that to you it does *not* seem strange, think hard! Do even you, who are Catholics, sometimes find it inhuman when a young boy leaves home and fatherland to offer himself as a missionary, to preach the Kingdom of God to nations who, denying Christ, still know not what they do? Or when a lovely girl, fresh and high-spirited, immures herself in a convent to offer her life, her days and nights of prayer, for thieves unknown and sinners unloved, that they too may one day be with Christ in paradise? Does it not seem strange that they should (so far as outward actions go) think first of those who hate them, or those whom they do not even know, and only then find time for parents and friends and lovers?

God has always acted this way with those whom He loves and that Christ should so act is another manifestation of the divinity of Him Who died on Calvary. God has always expected His saints to act this way and that the finest flower of His Church should so act is another proof of the identity with Christ of that Church which seems, even at times to its members, so strange and so inhuman in its demands.

We have seen the majestic dignity of Jesus on His Cross. Perhaps it were well here to remind ourselves that human sentiments, even human tears, were not inconsistent with the divine dignity of the Lord. The Scriptures recount that three times in His life Our Lord wept, but no tears of merely physical pain or personal frustration were these tears of Jesus. He wept for love of His friend at the tomb of Lazarus; He wept for love of His nation, gazing upon the doomed City of Jerusalem; He wept for love of God at the thought of the evil that brought Him to Calvary.

These last tears His Blessed Mother, adding tears for Him, shared on Calvary. But the tears of Mary, we must believe, are no less noble than those of her sacred Son whom she mirrored faithfully. In her, on Calvary, we may expect to find the fortitude and the majesty with which Jesus Himself drank the cup of sorrows to its utter emptying.

No one who knows mothers has been responsible for the tradition of the fainting Mother of Sorrows whom we encounter in so many pietistic paintings and books of baroque devotion. No one who has ever seen other mothers, far less perfect than she, take leave of their own flesh and blood at sailings for distant exile, at the departure of troop-trains, at open graves, can quite accept the picture of Mary which these provide. Men marvel at the strength of the mother of the persecuted Machabees, and they recognize other mothers in that valiant woman of whom the Scriptures tell: "She was to be admired above measure, and worthy to be remembered by all good men, who beheld her seven sons slain in one day, and bore it with good courage, for the hope that she had in God: and she bravely exhorted every one of them to remain faithful, being filled with wisdom, and joining a man's heart to a woman's thoughts."

Remembering these other mothers, we are relieved to find in the Gospel no hint of unbecoming grief in Mary, no word of moral or physical shrinking in that Mother whom Catholics hail as their advocate and their strength. Mary espoused the redemption in silence; she did not cry out; she is not named among the women who wept for her Son. We read in the Gospel only these movingly restrained words: "NOW THERE STOOD BY THE CROSS OF JESUS HIS MOTHER." "I read that she stood," says St. Ambrose, "I read nowhere that she wept." Yet . . . tears there doubtless were, silent tears, noble tears, tears like those of Christ whose co-sufferer she was.

Mary, despite her great grace and singular intimacy with Jesus, was still utterly human. Closely intimate was her knowledge of Christ; still she walked by faith in His divinity, a faith unmatched among men, but faith no less than ours.

We must not forget how different, as well as how alike, were the sufferings of Jesus and Mary. Now that His hour had come, Jesus, consoled by the Beatific Vision, the clear knowledge of God's Goodness and God's Truth which never ceased entirely to irradiate His human mind, could exult in His most agonizing sorrows at the thought of the early harvest of grace and glory which His sufferings would win. Mary, though sustained by faith more ardent than ever before, must have found herself on Calvary fighting fears more harrowing than she had ever known as she stood by the Cross of Jesus and gazed on flesh of her flesh, naked as the day she bore Him, mangled beyond a mother's power to heal.

The measure of Mary's grief is the measure of her love; and we who cannot equal the purity of the love of Mary for Jesus cannot realize the agony which the sight of His sufferings caused her. She loved Him as her own familiar friend because of the long and loyal common life she had shared with Him. She loved Him as a disciple might love an incomparable master for the sublime teaching she had received from Him. She loved Him as a perfect mother must love a son perfect in soul and beautiful in body. She loved Him as the Queen of all martyrs must love the God and Redeemer for whom countless martyrs, without ever seeing Him, have been willing to die and for whom countless Christian maidens, merely for having heard His Name, have been willing all the days of their lives to imitate the virginity of His Mother.

What must this daughter of Eve have suffered who, loving Jesus by these titles we can scarcely understand and with an intensity we can never measure, gathered together within the narrow space of a woman's fragile heart all the martyrdoms and all the torments which were dispersed over the body of Jesus, her Son! Even a mother, in order to appreciate Mary's affliction, would have to be as sensitive, because as pure, as Mary; as devoted, because as close to Jesus: yet only a mother may even guess the sorrow of Mary on Calvary.

But perhaps a man, a son, can feel something of the sympathy of Jesus for His mother. Outraged and dishonored, He saw the last person in the world who would wish Him this end gazing upon Him with unflinching loyalty. The sight of her reminded Him of past joys; in her grief she stood with women with whom she had once shared the happiness she found in Him, but women who now, far less than she, could hope to comprehend the mystery of iniquity which seemed to have brought Him—and His mother—to infamous confusion. He saw all pale and wasted that face once so like His own that just as He is called the Sun of Justice, so she is called its mirror. Hands which once had lifted Him, He saw now impotent to take Him down; hands which once had opened, simply and graciously, to greet Him, He saw now dry and twisted from unconscious clenching. Bent was the ivory tower of her queenly body, trembling the mystic rose of her virginal mouth, taxed to the limits of its endurance by a mother's compassion was her maternal courage. And seeing her pathetic efforts to share His dignity who shared His suffering, Jesus wept for His blessed mother.

O Jesus Christ, true Son of God and perfect Man, as sincerely as ever we thanked Thee for all the gifts of Thy creation, for all the graces of Thy redemption, we thank Thee for Thy tears. Never again shall we be ashamed to weep for those we love! Never shall we regret that we are as human as God's own Son, human. He, even at the apex of a work which only His divinity could do! Every tear that the innocent have shed in exile; every tear that the loving have shed in separation; every tear that a human being has shed in sorrow, in bewilderment—not Mary alone, but Jesus consecrated on Calvary when tears of Mary's Son mingled with blood that belonged to God in the laver that cleansed and redeemed us.

THE FOURTH WORD

And at the ninth hour, Jesus cried out with a loud voice, saying: Eloi, Eloi, lamma sabacthani? which is, being interpreted, *My God, My God, why hast Thou forsaken Me?* (Mark 15, 34).

What thoughts must have filled the mind of Jesus during those three hours of slow death on Calvary? Most writers would have us suppose that His human thoughts were in the future; some even suggest that, influenced by the position of His Cross (His enemies having deliberately crucified Him with His back to the East where lay Jerusalem and the scenes of His terrestrial life), the thoughts of Jesus flowed westward where the richest fruits of His passion would flourish, and especially, perhaps, to Rome, beyond the margin of the western sky, where new Peters, stronger than the first, would serve God's servants in another holy city set upon another hill destined to endure forever: a new Rome, so faithful to Christ whom the old Rome had crucified, that it would dare to call Him its First Citizen.

Well, no doubt, many of the thoughts of Christ were in the future. As His life ebbed, however, many things must have flooded back from the past on the tide of memory: all the human things He had known since coming into the world, all the divine things He had come into the world to do. No mere detail of the position of His Cross, no malicious scheme to blot out His homeland from His vision, could keep the eyes of Jesus, as finally they closed in death, from seeing with especial love the village street of Nazareth, the cherished scenes of His boyhood which had colored all of His teaching; the details of the market-place, the sheep-folds, the kitchen of His mother's humble home, the paternal watchfulness of Joseph; for all these He had woven into the little tapestries of Galilean life which are His parables. Memories of His mother Mary as she had been in the bloom of youth a quarter of a century before; Joseph—dead now and his shop silent; Elizabeth and His sturdy cousin John who was sanctified by Jesus before Jesus Himself was born, and who had died as a martyr for Jesus before Jesus Himself had come to dying. Persons . . . places . . . things, they all came streaming back. . . .

Had those days been happier than this terrible Friday? We may well doubt it. Today He is doing the work He has waited more than thirty years to do. Surely before this day no moment of His life could be completely satisfactory. There had always been that preoccupation with work-to-be-done: "Knew ye not that I must be about My Father's business?" There had been incessant reminders of the necessity of this work in every word He had heard, in every action He witnessed, in everything about Him,—tainted as all things were with sin, even the little children with their petty malice and their strange wilfulness.

He remembered, too, on Calvary all the saddening denials of His claim to be the Messias promised Israel. He remembered the day He had risen to read, as might any confirmed young man, the prophecies in the synagogue of His own hometown. The text that day was from Isaias, and it was so clearly of Him that the Prophet spoke that Jesus could not refrain from saying so. What an uproar that had caused! Some had wondered at His words of grace, but most were so angry that they rose up and cast Him out from their midst. . . .

He never went back there again. But day by day He lived out the letter of the prophecies. All His life He read them, re-read them, preached them—especially the psalms. Phrases from these sacred poems were constantly on His lips, and all of His life was unfolding as a successive fulfillment of the things they foretold, from the most glorious details of His life to the most harrowing.

No one of the prophets had pre-intoned the song of redemption as clearly and as movingly as had the Poet-King, His ancestor, David. Of all the psalms of David, one especially had been His favorite because it spoke so unmistakably of this day, this day, HIS day for which all of His life had been a preparation. He had not spoken much of this especially cherished psalm to His disciples; they were so easily scandalized, so lacking at times in spiritual insight. To them it might have seemed, as indeed it still does to some of His followers, a melancholy, strange, obscure psalm. It took its name, as did every psalm, from its opening words; they were: ELOI, ELOI, LAMMA SABACTHANI, My God, My God, why hast Thou forsaken Me?

It is to this psalm that our minds must turn if we would understand Christ's strange fourth word from the Cross. The psalmist, himself a type of the Messias, depicts a dream of desolation and torment at the hands of his enemies. He imagines himself as forsaken though still trusting in the God of his fathers, the God who had been with him from his infancy. Then in a series of dramatic images, the imagery of a nightmare, he suggests the horror of his plight: he dreams himself in the midst of a herd of wild beasts; their horns are lowered against him; their breath is hot upon his face. Then, nightmare-like, the imagery swiftly changes: he dreams himself a sick man at the point of death, too weak to protest as his dying eyes see greedy heirs massed about his bed, already dividing his possessions. As he struggles to free himself from this degrading image, his nightmare takes new and more frightening forms: he is now a timid animal around which hunting dogs have closed; he is a sheep torn in the maw of a marauding lion; suddenly he is a man again whose blood is flowing all about him like water on the ground; he is a man of wax, his enemies have discovered this and have kindled a fire beneath him; he melts; and now he is a skeleton, though somehow alive and able to feel and hear, as his foes touch each of his bones, calling out the number of them, one by one. One thought alone sustains this wretched man: God is his Father, and, somehow because of these torments, many brethren shall be raised up in freedom to the living God.

Jesus Christ lived out with excruciating fidelity every detail of David's sickening dream. Line by line the psalm of David was cadencing through His memory as He hung dying, and one by one the incidents of His passion realized its prophetic words: "I AM A WORM, AND NO MAN: THE REPROACH OF MEN AND THE OUTCAST OF THE PEOPLE." So sang the psalmist . . . and so Christ truly felt when, naked as a worm and stretched out of human semblance, repudiated by His people, He heard the passersby deride Him.

"ALL THEY THAT SAW ME HAVE LAUGHED ME TO SCORN: THEY HAVE SPOKEN WITH THE LIPS, AND WAGGED THE HEAD. HE HOPED IN THE LORD, LET HIM DELIVER HIM: LET HIM SAVE HIM, SEEING HE DELIGHTETH IN HIM." So sang the psalmist . . . and in the same consciousness with which He recalled the words. Christ was aware of the mob howling about Him, and of the mockery St. Matthew describes: "AND THEY THAT PASSED BY, BLASPHEMED HIM, WAGGING THEIR HEADS AND SAYING . . . 'IF HE BE THE KING OF ISRAEL, LET HIM COME DOWN FROM THE CROSS, AND WE WILL BELIEVE HIM. HE TRUSTED IN GOD: LET HIM DELIVER HIM NOW, IF HE WILL HAVE HIM.' " Christ thought of the lines: "MANY CALVES HAVE SURROUNDED ME: FAT BULLS HAVE BESIEGED ME . . ." and even as He did so, the hot breath of the fanatics who pressed close to molest and strike His helpless body soiled and burned His most pure flesh. A spasm of hemorrhages, and there flamed in His memory the words He had always known in His heart and now knew experimentally in every inch of His broken body: "I AM POURED OUT LIKE WATER; MY HEART IS BECOME LIKE WAX MELTING WITHIN ME; THEY HAVE DUG MY HANDS AND FEET; THEY HAVE NUMBERED ALL MY BONES." So may Christ number them Himself if His head but twist to the left or right and see His own torn and distended arms, or sink forward to gaze at His bruised ribs all but bursting through the taut, emaciated flesh still left to Him.

We should not now find it strange that this psalm, here so literally verified in its every grim detail, should have preoccupied the dying Christ; so preoccupied Him that He began to recite it aloud,—perhaps in the hope that those few who still lingered loyally near Him might see, as He did, how His very passion offered the final proof that He was the Messias so long foretold, so ardently desired; perhaps in the hope that they might take new heart on hearing Him cry forth with His last breath the paean of praise with which the psalm culminates:

"LET ALL THE SEED OF ISRAEL FEAR HIM: BECAUSE HE HATH NOT SLIGHTED NOR DESPISED THE SUPPLICATION OF THE POOR MAN. NEITHER HATH HE TURNED AWAY HIS FACE FROM ME: AND WHEN I CRIED TO HIM HE HEARD ME . . . THE POOR SHALL EAT AND BE FILLED: AND THEY SHALL PRAISE THE LORD THAT SEEK HIM: THEIR HEARTS SHALL LIVE FOREVER AND EVER. ALL

THE ENDS OF THE EARTH SHALL REMEMBER, AND SHALL BE CONVERTED TO THE LORD . . . TO HIM MY SOUL SHALL LIVE AND MY SEED SHALL SERVE HIM. THERE SHALL BE DECLARED TO THE LORD A GENERATION TO COME: AND THE HEAVENS SHALL SHOW FORTH HIS JUSTICE TO A PEOPLE THAT SHALL BE BORN, WHICH THE LORD HATH MADE."

Thus would Christ have spoken had He completed the psalm which He began with those choked words, "My God, My God, why hast Thou forsaken Me?" But even as He opened His sacred lips to speak, another and haunting verse of David's prophecy became verified; "MY STRENGTH IS DRIED UP . . . MY TONGUE HATH CLEAVED TO MY JAWS . . . THOU HAST BROUGHT ME DOWN INTO THE DUST OF DEATH. . . ."

And Jesus was heard to choke, and to cry, "I thirst."

THE FIFTH WORD

After this Jesus, knowing that all things were now accomplished, that the scripture might be fulfilled, said: *I thirst.*

(John 19, 28).

And immediately one of (the soldiers) running took a sponge, and filled it with vinegar: And put it on a reed, and gave him to drink. (Matthew 28, 48).

INRI

A burning thirst prevented the completion by Jesus of the solemn prophecy of His passion and redemptive death which the Poet-King had sung so many centuries before. It may be that by some association the lines of another psalm, also sung for Him by His type and prophet, David, ran through His feverish memory and forced to His lips the whispered plaint: "I thirst!" For David had also sung for Him the bitter line: "IN MY THIRST THEY GAVE ME VINEGAR TO DRINK."

Or it may be that, eager now for death, looking forward to an ecstasy now but moments removed, Jesus remembered the nostalgic aspiration of another psalm: "MY SOUL HATH THIRSTED AFTER THE STRONG, THE LIVING GOD: WHEN SHALL I COME AND STAND BEFORE THE FACE OF GOD?" Perhaps these lines gave to His lips the words: "I thirst!"

In either case, whether that dominant suffering was that of the soul thirsting after its Maker or that of a body parched by pain, this so tardy confession of His agony reveals the reality of Christ's suffering to the very end; the cry was immediately interpreted as a plea for help.

A plea for help from Jesus, the Son of God! Jesus asks a favor. It was a favor anyone could grant (the favors Christ continues to ask through those who plead in His name are still almost always favors anyone could grant); but only one man on Calvary chose to heed His cry.

When Jesus Christ was dying, when the Help of the helpless Himself cried out for help, the kings of the earth, the political men who, worthy or unworthy, share His sovereignty, were nowhere to be found. They were long since bored with Christ; they had dismissed Him from their busy minds. The representatives of the old religion were not there either or, if they were, they kept a prudent silence. Quite possibly they were afraid that they might be investigated for treason, disloyalty to Caesar, if they followed their own presumably more sensitive instincts and stood too close to a man condemned by the Law.

In any case, they were not there. It was a flippant soldier—suddenly grown tender-hearted—a young conscript under orders to do the vile work of Caesar, who obeyed a law more fundamental than Caesar's and offered Jesus the refreshing solace of a few drops of wine. It has frequently been somehow consoling to some of us in this sad period of our history that the one man on Calvary who helped Jesus to die was a common soldier.

The soldiers had beside them a vessel containing the wine rationed out to them for refreshment during the death-watch; it was a crude mixture, and sour; the Scriptures call it vinegar. One of them dipped a sponge in the wine and, fastening it to a bit of reed, pressed it close to the lips of Jesus. The Gospel says he went *running* to do this mercy, and the word suggests that he was young, perhaps one of the boys from the conquered provinces who made up Caesar's army of occupation. He may have been a young Gaul from what is now called France or a blond German lad from the region of the Rhine who suddenly forgot the disciplined hardness taught him by his officers and went running to do a kindness to the Crucified. Whoever he was, his youthful action brought to Calvary, so many miles from home, a trace of the gentleness of his nameless German, British, or Gallic mother.

If, like one of his commanders who protested his faith when Jesus finally had expired, this rude soldier ever came to understand the truth concerning Jesus,—ah, how he must have cherished ever afterward the memory of this moment! But even if Christ did not reveal His divinity to this young pagan, surely Christ never forgot the mercy done His humanity by the young soldier who offered a share of the best he had as a courtesy which Jesus accepted as such.

Lord Jesus, when our brothers, or sons, or friends who are soldiers, are lonesome for those who love them; when innocent soldiers, no matter what their flag, still sent to do the dark and dubious work of Caesar, cry out to you in pain or worry, then, Lord Jesus, remember that young soldier and how he tried to comfort as best he could the humanity You shared with him when You were sick unto death!

We have not emphasized the physical sufferings of Christ on Calvary, but this cry of pain reminds us not to forget them. The sufferings of His body were such that (the word is from prophecy) from the sole of His foot to the crown of His head there was no sound part in Him. He was not wounded, He was all one wound, one wound so monstrous that it left no trace of the comeliness that had made Him the most beautiful among the sons of men. His back lay open where the lash had done its hideous work (Lord Jesus, forgive my unbending pride!) His shoulders under the crushing weight of the cross had lost their shape (Jesus, forgive their misuse of my strength!) His chest, strained and disjointed, had all but crushed into silence His most adorable heart (Lord Jesus, forgive my lusts, my wayward love!) His bleeding head, weary with long waking, misshapen under blows, defiled with spittle and discharge, hung in unrecognizable distortion (cleanse me, Lord Jesus, of every sin of sight, of speech, of hearing, of thought!)

It is literally true that the depths of Christ's agony only God Himself could know. Yet even in the abyss of this degradation, how He surpasses in moral grandeur even the most resplendent of His saints! St. Francis, we are told, showed his selfless charity when he kissed a leper full on the mouth;

but Jesus was not content to embrace a leper with such passing union; Jesus Christ *became* the leper and *exchanged* His eternal life for the leper's dying flesh! How truly Jesus could say to Blessed Angela: " 'Twas in no jest that I have loved you! There is no sin, no disease of your soul for which I have not paid the penalty and provided the remedy by receiving the disease into My own fair flesh!"

Each of the Seven Words of Christ we cherish for some special reason. Some of the words, those in which He forgives and promises paradise, only a God could have uttered, and they send us to our knees in prayerful worship. Others—this word of thirsting pain is one—we may not fully understand, but we can understand them in part and so we cherish them as symbols of a sympathy between ourselves and Christ, a sympathy which carries with it, if not the full solution of certain human problems, at least the soothing of spirits tormented by the riddles of our destiny. It takes the sting from poverty, from pain, from sorrow, to find that in these, too, Christ conformed Himself to us. Is any poor? So was He. Is any sorrowful? So was He—even unto death. Is any in pain? So was He. Is any dying, crying out for a cooling sip of water? So was He. He touched our lives at every point, and whatever in them He touched He gave meaning, clarifying some of their obscure purposes, sanctifying their physical evil.

Christ did not remove the problem of evil from our lives, the physical evil of pain included. Christ did not even answer, in any dialectical sense, the problem of pain. But He did take the heartbreak out of evil and something of the mystery out of pain by identifying Himself with it, by finding a place for it in His perfect personality. We still do not know the answer to the problem of pain. But we do know that there was pain in Christ and that Christ is the solution of all difficulties, the resolution of all doubts.

The Atonement, with its paradox of perfect humanity afflicted by pain, is a tremendous mystery. Yet the Cross unlocks more mysteries than it creates. Man considers all the pain and anguish of the world, and he says: "God cannot be good, He cannot be love and still look upon all this. Even God's heart would break!" The Church points to the Cross and answers: "God so loved the world as to send His only-begotten Son . . . *and His Son's heart did break!"*

THE SIXTH WORD

Jesus, therefore, when He had taken the vinegar, said: *It is consummated.* (John 19, 30).

INRI

By accepting the slight refreshment which a little wine afforded Him, Our Lord gave a clue that the end of His passion was drawing near. For just as He had refused to enter upon His agony with senses drugged by the drugging wine which executioners offered those about to be crucified, so now He begged a sip of wine to revive Him a little lest He conclude His agony with senses in complete remissness. The sip of wine restored for a moment His wavering consciousness, so necessary for clear thought and full consent. It required sufficient reflection and full consent of the will to commit the sins which nailed Christ to the Cross, and both were needed again for the action whereby those sins were to be cancelled out. So it was with keen aliveness, performing a fully human act, that Jesus tasted death for every man! "It is consummated," He cried. And in a few moments Jesus was dead.

IT IS CONSUMMATED! What did Jesus mean? Certainly He did not wish merely to indicate that the pain was done. It was not the cry of a weary sufferer welcoming rest. It was not in any sense complaint that life had been bitter and hard and that He was relieved to have it over with at last. It was not the cry of exhaustion, but the cry of triumph. Jesus Christ loved life; no word is more frequently on His lips than the word "life," and He was dying that men might have life and have it more abundantly. So when Christ cried, "It is consummated," He meant not that life, least of all His own life, was finished, but that *death* had ended and would be no more, and that life was just beginning for all the souls of men. Had this cry come as the most hushed whisper, had it been inaudible to all save to the God within Him, this cry for which the angels had listened from the the dawn of time and the holy souls from the dawn of history,—this cry, had it been only whispered, would have made the waiting heavens resound with ringing joy.

Two facts immediately impress us about this sixth utterance of Christ from the Cross. The first is that it is contained in a single word of the Greek from which our versions are made. In no pompous declaration was the supreme event of human history announced: in one word it was proclaimed that the salvation of man had been accomplished forever!

The second fact is that this word was uttered with a loud cry: it manifested Christ's consciousness of victory, not defeat. His had been a great destiny to accomplish: He had brought God to man in His Incarnation; now, having removed all obstacles thereto, He was bringing man back to God. The earth had been enriched with the heavenly dew for which Isaias yearned: "RORATE, COELI, DESUPER ET NUBES PLUANT JUSTUM: DROP DOWN DEW, YE HEAVENS, FROM ABOVE, AND LET THE CLOUDS RAIN DOWN THE JUST ONE: LET THE EARTH OPEN AND BUD FORTH A SAVIOUR!"

At the Incarnation the clouds of heaven had, so to speak, drenched the earth with life-giving grace, and out of it there had sprung, budlike, its Saviour; a Saviour who, again in the words of Isaias, had grown up as a tender plant, as a root out of thirsty ground. And now, having waxed strong and full of redemptive grace, this Saviour, clinging vinelike against the Cross, reached eagerly up to Heaven to grasp the Father's forgiving hand, the while all Heaven cried triumphantly: " 'Tis done! The pledge has been redeemed! The curse is lifted! The work is finished! And Christ is coming home!"

For there on Calvary . . .
". . . stretching out to earth's remotest bounds
His sacred arms, He brought the human race
From every clime, and gathering them in one,
As many as would cleave to Him,
He placed them in the very arms of God. . . ."

But was that victory so complete? Even now, after two thousand years, do we seem so much nearer the reign of Christ than were our forefathers centuries ago? The powers of evil sometimes seem so unrebuked. Still the Church prays: *Thy Kingdom come!* And still the mood of the Church is that of Advent, a patient, disciplined expectation of the perfect coming of the Kingdom.

Then, so far as earth goes, what was *finished* there on Calvary? Well, first of all, the tragic isolation of earth from Heaven was ended; the earth had been kindled again with fire let down from Heaven, a fire that would burn, and purge, and forge a new earth and a new Heaven. Then, Christ had proposed an ideal to a world incapable of dreaming, by itself, any part of such vision. He had called together a priestly group to preach this ideal, a group united by a vocation which could have stemmed only from Him, which could not have conceivably come about from chance encounters, human hoping, or planning or striving together. He had founded a Church to perpetuate His ideal and bring it one day to realization, a Church which, without Him, could no more have arisen and developed from the historical environment in which it began than a tropical garden could spring out of powdered stone. These things, the Gospel tells us, Jesus began to do and to teach.

In Heaven a plan had been decreed and His was the part to place that plan in operation among men; on earth He had made the beginning of its execution. He had made a *beginning,* but let not that word deceive you into minimizing the tremendous difference in human affairs that the smallest beginning made by Christ must necessarily entail. It was a beginning like Creation itself; where before was emptiness, void, now there is everything. It was a beginning as dawn is a beginning: where before there was naught but darkness, now all is light and high noon is inevitable. Once Christ has begun His work, all things must find their place in that work, or die. So things can never be the same again, as if the Crucifixion had not happened; the earth has been reborn and purified as after the great flood. Evil, violence, brutality, sin—all these may stay on, but they stay as relics of an order which every Christian knows is doomed unto utter extinction. Virtue, order, peace, love—these may be still inchoate, still eclipsed by their opposites, still tentative, but every Christian knows that to these belong the future. They are the dynamic realities, however long a time may be required to insure their triumph. They shall possess the earth: that fact is certain, for all things needed to effect their fullest ripening have been finally achieved on Calvary.

Henceforth there shall be no defeat for Christ.

Yet Calvary must be relived in every soul until all shall have made their peace with Him.

> "I saw the Son of Man go by
> Crowned with the crown of thorn.
> Was it not finished, Lord, I said,
> And all the anguish borne?
> He turned on me His awesome eyes,
> 'Hast thou not understood?
> Lo! Every soul is Calvary,
> And every sin a Rood.' "

The Kingdom of Heaven cometh not with observation; the signs of its coming are few and the vigil for it wearies all save the stout of heart. But be not cast down. Freshened by the blood of Christ the cold earth grows warm again; the grey world turns to green; the winter is now past; the rain is over and gone. Flowers have appeared in our land; now is the sure season of planting.

Colleges dedicated to learning Christ, convents to loving Him, blossom like springtime throughout the world. Unseen now and silent, year in, year out, the Sower goes forth to scatter seed. Still the seed falls often on hearts too hardened to respond. Sometimes the sprouts that give early promise wither as the seed encounters hidden rocks. Still falls some seed on soil in which, for lack of careful husbandry, weeds and briars and thorns choke out its growth. Still, too, however, His Church bears increasing fruit for Him; His seed yields a hundredfold as parishes radiating His life still flourish, schools propagating His truth grow great. Little by little, in patience and prayer, the granaries of God are filled with a harvest of heroic souls and virgin hearts, of hallowed learning and burning zeal—all contributing in their several ways to hasten the hour when the Lord of the harvest may go forth to claim His own, to reap the fruits of the seed that was sowed on Calvary. Then shall the angels echo back the cry of Christ from the Cross: "IT IS CONSUMMATED, THE EARTH IS THE LORD'S, THE LAMB HAS NOT BEEN SLAIN IN VAIN!"

THE SEVENTH WORD

And Jesus crying out with a loud voice, said: *Father, into Thy hands I commend My spirit.*

(Luke 23, 46).

Whatever trial of human nature may have echoed in the cry, "My God, My God, why hast Thou forsaken me?"; whatever passing torment of His human soul it may have reflected, all these are gone as Christ proclaims that His work is done, that torment now need be no more and that His trial is forever ended. The Divinity in Him cries out aloud that name of God which He alone has the natural right to employ: *Father.* "Father, into Thy hands I commend My spirit!"

O never-to-be-forgotten words! To how many martyred lives they have brought release since first Christ consecrated them! The holy deacon, Stephen, echoed them in Jerusalem of old, crying: "Lord Jesus, receive my spirit!" To how many weary days have these words brought repose as saintly priests and laymen have pronounced them in affectionate repetition at Compline, the beautiful office with which the Church closes her day of prayer: "IN MANUS TUAS, DOMINE, COMMENDO SPIRITUM MEUM . . . IN MANUS TUAS, DOMINE, COMMENDO SPIRITUM MEUM!" "Into Thy hands, O Lord, I commend my spirit."

The two last utterances of the Saviour followed one another in rapid succession. First, that in which, with a voice reborn of His restored physical strength, Christ exultantly proclaimed that His work, so far as the heaping up of merit is concerned, was done. Then His prediction of His own approaching death—uttered not with the voice of one expiring, but with the heroic voice of one giving life to the world. It was not Death that approached Christ, but Christ who approached Death. Death was afraid of Christ. So Christ bowed His head and bade Death draw near, the Death needed that we might have Life.

His last cry, "with a loud voice," was not like the cry of one dying; it so moved the commander of the soldiery that, rude man and insensible to suffering as he must have been, he became frightened by the enormity of what he had done. He cried out: "Indeed this man was the Son of God!"

Yet on the threshold of His glory Jesus Christ retained the simplicity of a child. His very last words were words any child might have used. They were the words of a prayer which thirty years before in Nazareth He had learned at His mother's knee when, like any little Jewish boy, He made His evening prayer: *"Father, into Thy hands I commend my spirit."*

Impressive as is the simplicity of Christ's death when we concentrate our attention upon it alone, it is entirely consistent with the general tenor of His life; and this is the first teaching of the seventh word for us. Granting the exceptional and tremendous changes that may occur in the spiritual dispositions of a man about to die (changes due to utterly gratuitous last-minute graces granted by God, as in the case of the Good Thief), is it not still true that the vast majority of people appear to die just as they have lived? No deep interior revolution is normally to be expected as the last hour approaches. Those who have lived with indifference to God's grace generally take leave of life in that same disposition of indifference. Those who have lived in vigorous anticipation of the life to come die, as did a famous writer, crying: "Now for the great adventure!" Those who have lived preoccupied with self and property, with the little world they have built for themselves, go into eternity with a backward glance, eyes fixed hungrily upon the shore that is fading from sight. Those who have lived as pilgrims and strangers on the face of the earth, homesick for heaven all the days of their life, die, as did a saintly prelate, murmuring: "Now we are bound for home! At last we are going home!" Those who have dreamed away Time in a kind of spiritual lethargy are rarely bestirred to spiritual energy at the dawn of Eternity. The Holy Spirit whom they have resisted and misprized during life will not force their wills at the hour of death. The Tempter seems to leave them as they are; any last minute assault of Satan, if it upset them, might shatter the false complacency that makes them his. There is no necessary relationship between the quality of a man's life and the quality of his death, for the graces of God are bestowed according to the inscrutable good pleasure of God alone; God can, and sometimes does, effect a total conversion in the last split-second of a man's thinking and willing. Ordinarily, however, death matches life and proves to be only its last phase, and consistent with it in character. To assume that matters may be otherwise is to be guilty of presumption, one of the two alternative sins against the virtue of Hope.

On the heartening side, however, the man who has been accustomed through life to walk constantly in the presence of God, who has sincerely striven ever to do all things in God, and through God, and unto God, whose prayer has been "Thy Kingdom come,"—such a one is already so directed toward heaven that the transition from earth to paradise is almost incidental. For him there will be, there need be, no final frantic turn to God as the end approaches. He will conclude his life just as he would close a favorite book, turn down the light and climb the stairs. With him there will be no startled cry, no stupefaction, when he beholds the Room he has entered unawares. He will be perfectly at home with God, hereafter as here below. He will arrive already part of Heaven and with Heaven already part of him. For just as the love of earthly things makes us earthly; as the love of vile things makes us vile; as the food we eat becomes our very substance; as all men become the things they love: so the love of Heaven makes us heavenly, the love of God makes us somehow divine.

To those who have lived the life of grace Heaven will be no strange state; it will not be a new life but an intensification of the grace-life already present in them; a quickening to ecstasy of the tempo of their love, the same love with which on earth they sought the Face of God. His truth and beauty they have seen in time as through a mirror, darkly; now they gaze enraptured on God Himself, face-to-face for all eternity.

Christ, the God-Man, died as He had lived, the Perfect Son of God, and His last word is not different from His first, or from any intervening word. It was merely a culminating expression of that submission to His Father's Will which had been His sole preoccupation in word and work. It was a succinct formula that gathered together in matchless unity all of the desires, decisions, and actions of the most perfect life that men have ever seen, that God could show us.

So, in this last word there is a profound lesson

for us who seek to order our so complicated, so troubled, so dangerously varied modern lives.

The lesson is really very simple, though it took the whole life of Christ to teach it, and our own lives are far too short to learn it well. And the lesson is this: perfection is not in the mere knowledge of God's order but in submission to it. The order of God, the good pleasure of God, the will of God, —all these are one and the same thing in this life. What else is perfection but the faithful cooperation of the soul with the will of God? It was not by His knowledge that Christ saved us, though in Him were all the abysses of wisdom. It was by His submissive will: "HE BECAME OBEDIENT . . . WHEREFORE HATH GOD EXALTED HIM AND HATH GIVEN HIM A NAME WHICH IS ABOVE EVERY NAME."

Only by the imitation of Christ in His conformity to the will of God can the Kingdom of Heaven be realized in the world and the peace of Christ be diffused in men and nations. There is never peace for those who resist God; but the peace those win for themselves who submit to God is a contagious peace that spreads itself and Him throughout all of society. No man ever truly gave himself to Christ without some other's finding Christ through him; there is no life so hidden that, if it be sincere and humble and holy, God does not use it to shed light on the world and thus bring to pass, little by little, His sovereign will in the world: that will which is our peace.

That is why resignation to the will of God is the way to glory, not to defeat. The life of Christ should have taught us that. Most assuredly His death does. The life of Christ in the Church should teach us the same thing. "I make no distinction between Our Lord and His Church," said St. Joan of Arc, "They are all one!"

And so, if, as is claimed, Christ in His Church is due to suffer again because of the refusal of men to hear Him, when that persecution breaks Catholics will see in it the sign of glory, not the sign of defeat. Indeed, when the Church is courted and fawned upon, when the Church is prosperous, it is usually not unreasonable to feel that her true point is being missed, that momentarily she is tasting defeat, just as the purposes of Christ, saluted with sanguine hosannas on Palm Sunday, were being mistaken by the mob. But frequently when the Church is being persecuted, when her blood spills, she is doing her real work, and is nearest her hour of triumph; just as Christ dying on Calvary, pouring out His life-stream, drop by drop, far from being defeated, was then truly and at last accomplishing the work which brought Him into this world.

There is no difference between Christ and His Church. They are all one. So through the Church Christ, though dead, still speaketh; through the Church He still forgives those who know not what they do; through the Church He still promises Paradise to those who come to Him with faith, hope, and charity; through the Church He still brings men under Mary's sheltering care, and wins for His Mother the jealous guardianship by the devout of the virtues which she embodies; through the Church He still calls out His Messianic rights and proclaims His final triumph; through the Church He still thirsts for prayers for His suffering dead, for His destitute living; through the

Church He still sees His work brought to fruition in each lonely soul, in each new corner of the world; through the Church He still proclaims the sovereignty of God, the lesson that in His Father's will lies every human hope in life and in death.

There was a moment, though, when Christ Himself tasted death in testimony to these lessons. There was darkness over all the earth . . . the sun was darkened and the veil of the temple was split asunder . . . the earth quaked . . . and, bowing His head, Jesus died.

O beautiful obedience of His low-bowed head. O boundless charity of His outstretched arms. O dear dead human hands so torn with toil! . . . And over all the awful silence, the perfect peace, the utter majesty of Deity. . . .

O God Our Father, gaze on the countenance of Thine Anointed One, now dead for us! RESPICE, DOMINE, IN FACIEM CHRISTI TUI! Gaze, O Lord, on the face of Thy Christ! Recognize in its majesty traces of the Divinity which He shares with Thee, and in the humility of His broken body see how He is also one of us!

He is God of Thy Substance, but also Man of ours: Thy Son and our Brother; RESPICE, DOMINE, IN FACIEM CHRISTI TUI! Gaze, O Lord, on the face of Thy Christ and spare His people whose flesh He wore, in whose flesh He suffered, whose flesh He died to sanctify, whose words in pain are the penalty of our sins, the pledge of our redemption.

We adore Thee, O Christ, and we bless Thee!

Because by Thy Holy Cross Thou hast redeemed the world!